ANIMALS

Christopher McHugh

Thomson Learning
New York

Discovering Art

Cover The Purple Fox *painted by the German artist Franz Marc. Heydt Museum, Wuppertal, Germany.*

First published in the
United States in 1993 by
Thomson Learning
115 Fifth Avenue
New York, NY 10003

First published in 1992 by
Wayland (Publishers) Limited
61 Western Road, Hove
East Sussex BN3 lJD
England

Library of Congress Cataloging-in-Publication Data
McHugh, Christopher.
        Animals / Christopher McHugh.
                p.   cm. --(Discovering art)
        Includes bibliographical references and index.
        Summary: A brief examination of the ways artists from all over the world and
throughout history have portrayed animals in their art.
        ISBN 1-56847-025-8 : $14.95
        1. Animals in art--Juvenile art. 2. Art--Juvenile literature. [1. Animals in art. 2. Art
appreciation.] I. Title. II. Series.
N7660.M38 1993
704.9'432--dc20   92-43265

Printed in the United States of America

Contents

1 Animals in art

People have always liked to make animals a subject of art. They have been drawn, painted, and sculpted from ancient times to the present day. Why have animals always been such a popular subject? In this book you can find some of the reasons.

The carved animals on a totem pole, made by Native Americans, may represent the animal spirits that protect the tribe. Enormous carved stone lions may stand at the gate of a palace to scare away enemies. In a painting, animals may illustrate the Bible story of how God created

1 Tropical storm with tiger *by Henri Rousseau, reproduced by courtesy of the Trustees, The National Gallery, London.*

the world full of living creatures. You can see pictures of the Garden of Eden on pages 11 and 12, painted by two different artists, that illustrate this story.

Picture **1** (opposite) is like a modern version of the Garden, but here it is shown as a wild and violent place. Picture **2** (above) shows beautiful leopard sculptures from West Africa. They were made from ivory and bronze.

Animals can be shown, in art, as friendly or frightening. They can be funny or grand. They can look realistic, or be changed so much that they seem to be only a pattern. They can be shown as the size they are in life, or smaller, or larger. They can be the animals we know or the strange creatures found only in stories.

2 *Sculptures of a pair of ivory leopards from Benin, West Africa. British Museum, London.*

5

2 An ancient beginning

The animal kingdom has been continuously changing since far back in the mists of time. Over thousands of years, a certain kind of ape grew to be different from the other animals. Not only did it walk on two legs and use stones as tools, but its head was a slightly different shape, with room for a larger brain. Time passed and the apes began to do strange things, such as arranging stones in patterns and scratching shapes in the dirt. These were the first people. After several thousands of years they were painting beautiful pictures on rocks and in caves.

Picture **3** is one of their paintings, and as you can see, it shows an animal–a bison. It can be quite surprising to see how accurate and beautiful these paintings are.

3 *A cave painting of a bison, made thousands of years ago. It is in a cave at Altameira, in Spain.*

We do not know exactly why prehistoric people made their pictures. Perhaps the paintings helped them to feel sure of catching an animal in the hunt. Or perhaps they believed the animals were some kind of gods.

As time went by, people began to organize themselves into groups or societies. One of the first of these societies was in the area now called the Middle East. The ancient Greeks called this region Mesopotamia, meaning land between the rivers. Picture **4** is a work of art from Mesopotamia. The goat is made with gold and other precious materials, and it shows how skilled the ancient craftsmen became.

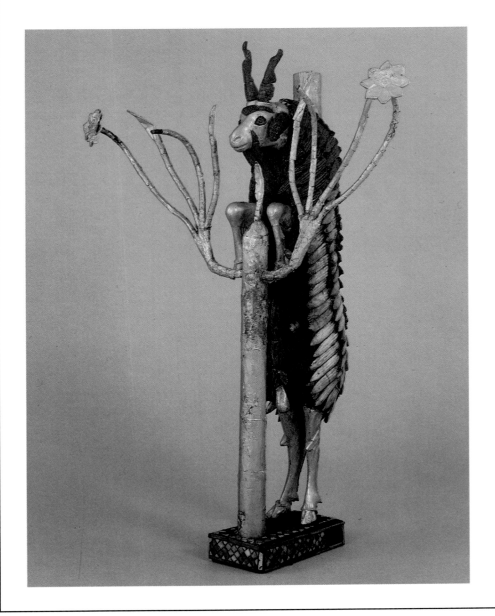

4 Goat in a thicket, *from Southern Mesopotamia. This ornament is about six thousand years old. British Museum, London.*

7

3 Animals in the ancient world

We can get a very good idea of what life was like for the ancient Egyptians from the remains of their buildings and the works of art inside them. We see that animals played an important part in both their everyday and religious lives. Many of their gods were part animal. Picture **5** shows the top of a vase made in the shape of a falcon, a bird they believed was sacred.

Life in Egypt was centered along the valley of the Nile River. The river provided the water that allowed the people to grow crops and raise animals. Domestic animals like those we know today, such as dogs and cats, often had to do a share of the work. The cat in the wall painting, picture **6**, is helping the hunter to catch birds.

The Ancient Greeks lived in the islands and coastlands of the Aegean Sea, in the southeastern corner of Europe. They borrowed ideas from the cultures of Mesopotamia

5 *The top of a vase with the head of a falcon, from the royal tomb at Tanis in Egypt. Egyptian Museum, Cairo.*

6 Fowling in the marshes, *an Egyptian wall painting from the tomb at Nebamun, Thebes. British Museum, London.*

7 *A Greek sculpture of horsemen—part of the Parthenon Friez, from the Acropolis in Athens. British Museum, London.*

and Egypt. They also developed their own style of art. Myths were very important to the Greeks, and although these were always stories about people and gods, animals often appeared in them too.

Picture 7 shows a sculpture that formed part of a temple wall on the Acropolis in Athens. The sculpture was made by carving the shapes into a slab of stone–this is called a "relief sculpture." The Greeks were very skilled at carving figures and animals realistically. They could also carve them in a way that showed movement, as if the animals and people might be alive. Horses were especially important to them; it was on horseback that their ancestors had come to Greece hundreds of years earlier, from the plains of Asia.

The city-dwellers of Greece and Rome were never cut off from the sea or the countryside. So land and sea animals were important in their religion and mythology.

8 *A bronze sculpture of the she-wolf suckling Romulus and Remus. Etruscan Museum, Rome.*

A famous Roman myth tells the story of the twins Romulus and Remus. They were left, as babies, to drown in a basket in the Tiber River. They were saved by a she-wolf who fed them with her milk. When they grew up they planned to build a city. They argued over the plan, and Romulus killed his brother. Romulus went on to build the city which took its name from his: Rome. Picture **8** shows a bronze sculpture of the two young boys feeding from the she-wolf.

9 Dionysus riding on a leopard, *a mosaic from Delos in Greece.*

Most of the gods and goddesses of ancient Rome were borrowed from the Greeks. They were given Roman names; for instance, Zeus was named Jupiter, Aphrodite became Venus, Artemis was Diana. The Romans also borrowed the Greek ways of making art. In picture **9**, Dionysus, whose Roman name was Bacchus, is riding on the back of a leopard. Dionysus was the Greek god of wine and festivals. The picture is a mosaic; it was found on the Greek island of Delos. A mosaic is a picture made by gluing small pieces of colored stone or glass onto a floor or a wall.

4 Animals in the Creation

In most of the world's religions, the story that tries to explain how the world began is very important. The Christian version of the story of the Creation is based on the ancient writings known as the Bible. Yahweh, or God, created light, the sky, the earth and seas, plants and trees, sun, moon and stars, fish, birds, and animals. Finally he created Adam and Eve, the first man and woman.

At first all was well, and creatures and people lived together happily in the Garden of Eden. But then Adam and Eve broke Yahweh's rules. This ended the time of peace, and brought suffering and death into the world. Picture **10** shows a painting of the Garden of Eden by the Flemish artist Jan Brueghel. His father and his brother were painters too.

10 The Garden of Eden *by the Flemish artist Jan Brueghel. Victoria and Albert Museum, London.*

There are many paintings of the Garden of Eden. The idea of an unspoiled world of animals and people living together in peace is very attractive. It expresses how perfect and beautiful life might be. Picture **11** was painted by an American artist, Edward Hicks, who was also a preacher. His painting of *The Peaceable Kingdom*, where animals and people all live happily together, is his way of suggesting a better world that people should try to achieve.

Picture **12** shows a painting by Antonio Pisanello. This describes a story about a Christian saint. While he was out hunting, St. Eustace came across a stag that was bearing a glowing crucifix between its antlers. The stag was bringing a message to the saint from God.

It is interesting to see the differences between this picture and the other pictures of hunts in this book, for example on pages 17, 18, and 19.

11 The Peaceable Kingdom *by Edward Hicks, Philadelphia Museum of Art, Pennsylvania.*

12 The Vision of Saint Eustace *by Antonio Pisanello, courtesy of The National Gallery, London.*

5 Animals in art around the world

There is so much art showing animals from all over the world that it was difficult to know which to choose for this book. The following pages will show you just a few.

Picture **13** is a Chinese painting on silk, showing monkeys in a fruit tree. The soft colors and delicate drawing are typical of many Chinese paintings.

These drawings (below) are in the Northern Territory in Australia. They were made by the Aboriginal people, who have always expressed their mythology with paintings and drawings, on the ground, on rocks, or on pieces of bark. Animals, like the kangaroos in picture **14**, are an important part of their lives.

13 Pipa (fruit) and Monkey; *a painting on silk from China. National Palace Museum, Taiwan.*

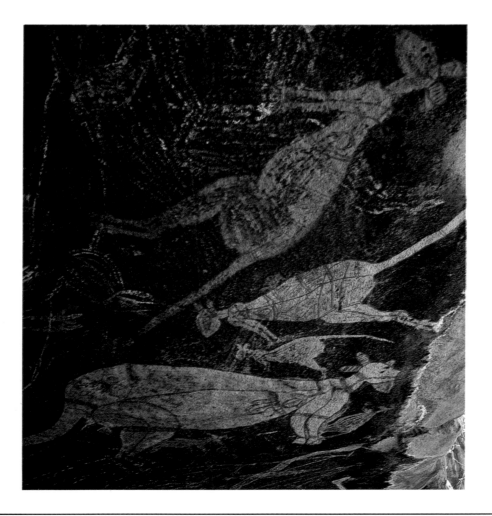

14 *Aboriginal rock paintings, from Christmas Caves, South Alligator River Area, Australia.*

15 *The title of this Indian miniature is* Royal Sports at Agra. *Victoria and Albert Museum, London.*

Picture **15** is an Indian miniature, painted in the 1600s. It shows a scene with different sports going on. You can see that the artist has laid the figures around the picture in a flat pattern.

16 *Totem poles in Stanley Park, western Canada*

When the Europeans arrived in America in the 1500s, they found civilizations already there–the original peoples of America whom they called Indians.

The North American continent is huge. The land varies tremendously. There are mountains, plains, deserts, forests, jungles, swamps, and islands. The Native Americans living there were all different, depending on what region of the continent they lived in. Each group or tribe had to adapt to the different land and climates.

Picture **16** shows the totem poles of Native Americans from the northwest coast of North America. It shows the carved and brilliantly colored animal spirits that are the emblems of their tribe. Many tribes still use animal shapes as their emblems.

17 *An Inuit mask from southeast Alaska, representing the soul of a salmon.*

18 *A temple carving made by the Zapotec people, from Monte Alban, Mexico.*

Picture **17** is an Inuit mask from Alaska. The mask shows a fish and the strange human-like face of its spirit. Animal spirits are very important to most Native Americans. To them, the spirits show how the world came to be created and how the forces of nature continue to work together.

Picture **18** is a figure carved on a stone slab. It comes from an ancient temple built by the Zapotec people, in an area which is today part of Mexico. The figure is drawn by cutting a line into the flat stone. There are hundreds of these carved slabs. They probably show the animal spirits of people who have died. This one seems to be a monkey. Contrast this with picture **7** on page 9 to see how different stone carvings can be in style, technique, and feeling.

6 Animals in European art

The Middle Ages is the name given to the period in Europe between the end of the Roman Empire and the Renaissance (from about A.D. 500 to 1500). The years from about 500 to 1000 are sometimes called the Dark Ages. It was a time of violence and confusion in Europe.

The Vikings came from the north, attacking and plundering villages.Picture **19** is the figurehead from a Viking longboat. These ships were long and narrow, built for speed. They carried the Viking raiders into foreign lands and home again with their booty. The Vikings believed that monstrous figureheads, like this one with its ferocious mouth, would terrify their victims and the spirits that protected them.

20 *An ivory carving showing hunting and harvesting. Bargello Museum, Florence, Italy.*

19 *The figurehead on the prow of a Viking longboat.*

Through the Middle Ages, life in Europe gradually became more organized. Different groups of people arrived from the north and east to settle in farms and villages, and they produced new kinds of art. Picture **20**, on page 17 (overleaf), is a beautiful ivory carving showing scenes of hunting and harvesting. Ivory carvings like this were popular with many of these newly settled peoples, including the Saxons in England and the Lombards in Italy.

Although at this time most art was made for the Church, the Devonshire tapestry (picture **21**) was made at the end of the Middle Ages, when nonreligious subjects were beginning to become popular. In this picture showing part of a tapestry, the people, animals, and trees are arranged in a pattern. You might overlook the bears and the dogs at first. This arrangement is done similarly to the way the Indian miniature is painted (picture **15**) on page 14.

21 Detail from the Devonshire Tapestries. *Victoria and Albert Museum, London.*

A hunt is also the subject of the painting by Uccello, in picture **22**. It was painted in Italy during the period known as the Renaissance. Renaissance means rebirth; it was the time when earlier Greek and Roman ideas were rediscovered and became popular. Look at this picture and then compare it with picture **1**. You can see how the artists have each shown that some things are nearer and some farther away.

Picture **23** by Albrecht Dürer is a woodcut of a rhinoceros, then a very unusual animal in Europe. The ideas of the Renaissance spread from Italy throughout

22 A Hunt in a Forest *by Paolo Uccello. Ashmolean Museum, Oxford.*

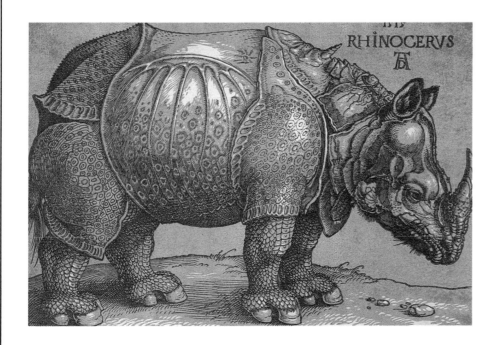

23 *A woodcut showing a rhinoceros, by Albrecht Dürer. British Museum, London.*

Europe. Dürer was one of the first German artists to understand the new ideas about making pictures. Like many Renaissance artists, he was fascinated by the world around him. He made many drawings, paintings, and prints to find out more about it.

During the Renaissance people became interested in portraits. Many people wanted to have their portraits painted, and some artists made a fortune by painting

24 Charles I on Horseback
*by Sir Anthony Van Dyck,
reproduced by courtesy of the
Trustees, The National
Gallery, London.*

20

them. Sir Anthony Van Dyck was one. He was born in Flanders, which is part of present-day Belgium. But his greatest success was as a portrait painter in England, at the court of King Charles I. Picture **24** is a portrait of Charles on a horse. This was a popular form of portrait, called an equestrian portrait. This kind of picture was meant to make the person in the portrait seem very important.

Picture **26** shows people and animals in a peaceful country scene. Aelbert Cuyp was also a Dutch painter, just 21 years younger than Van Dyck. But the subjects of these two artists' paintings are very different. Look at both pictures and try to decide what you think are the most important differences.

25 A Milkmaid and Cattle near Dordrecht *by Aelbert Cuyp, reproduced by courtesy of the Trustees, The National Gallery, London.*

26 A Hound and a Bitch in a Landscape *by George Stubbs. The Tate Gallery, London.*

Dutch artists, in the 1600s, painted pictures in a style that was later copied in other countries. In England people liked paintings of certain subjects that were also popular with Dutch people. These subjects included the countryside (landscape) and everyday activities (genre). George Stubbs, an English artist in the 1700s, was influenced by Dutch paintings. He was famous for his paintings of animals, especially horses. Unlike some other pictures, which may amuse or entertain us, or show power, anger, or fear, Stubbs painted exactly what he saw. Picture **26** shows us a detailed painting of two dogs. Look at the animals in pictures **24**, **25**, and **26** to compare Stubbs' way of painting animals with that of Van Dyck or Cuyp.

Another great painter of horses was the French artist Théodore Géricault. Picture **27** shows his famous painting of a horse frightened by lightning during a thunderstorm. Like Stubbs, Géricault painted horses with a great love for their shape and their general appearance and grace of movement. See how he has captured the look of the horse's shiny coat. Géricault died young–in a horse-riding accident–but he was one of the first and best known painters of the Romantic Age, at the beginning of the 1800s. This was a time when artists (and writers and musicians too) liked to produce art that was filled with a feeling and love for nature. The horse's fear shows clearly in his startled posture and rolling eye.

27 A Horse frightened by Lightning *by Théodore Géricault, reproduced by courtesy of the Trustees, The National Gallery, London.*

7 Animals in the nineteenth century

The two pictures here are of paintings made in the nineteenth century. It is interesting to compare them because they show two very different feelings toward animals. The painting by English artist Sir Edwin Henry Landseer, picture **28**, was made with oil paint. Picture **29** is from a book of prints by John James Audubon, an American artist and naturalist. Audubon usually worked on paper with pen, pencil, and watercolor.

29 Tulip-tree, *one of many detailed illustrations from* Birds of America, *published in 1838, by John James Audubon. The British Library, London.*

The two artists have used different media (a word to describe different paints and techniques) and they had different ideas in mind. Landseer's picture has a title, *Dignity and Impudence*, which tells us about the animals' feelings (of importance and cheekiness). The dogs seem almost human. Audubon's picture, however, tells us nothing about feelings. It illustrates as exactly as possible the type of tree and species of bird.

Now look more closely at how the artists have painted the pictures. Audubon has used clear, careful outlines to describe the shapes of tree and birds. He has used color to fill in the shapes.

Landseer, on the other hand, has used soft outlines and plenty of light and shadow. He has used color mainly to indicate light and to show the different textures. Look at the large dog's eyes and nose for example, and the small dog's hair. Landseer felt very emotional about animals, and used paint to give them personality and character.

8 Modern animals

The twentieth century has been called the Modern period of art. It has been a time of enormous change: automobiles, telephones, airplanes, television, robots, computers, nuclear power, space travel. . . . Artists, as you might expect, have reacted to these fantastic changes.

Like artists before them, modern artists use animals in their art, showing them in different ways. Animals are often used to suggest what an artist's thoughts or feelings are about other people or the world. *The Purple Fox* by Franz Marc, on the cover of this book, shows an animal as a pure form of life, as opposed to people, who Marc thought were unkind, mean, and deceitful.

The painting by Pablo Picasso, picture **30**, shows a complicated relationship between people and animals. Bullfighting is a very ancient form of spectacle, still enjoyed among Mediterranean peoples. Picasso has woven

30 The Bull Fight: The Death of the Bull *by Pablo Picasso. Musee Picasso, Paris. © DACS, London 1992.*

the shapes of the bull, horse, and man together. The horse is caught between the power and wildness of the bull and the skill of the man. Picasso felt that the relationship between the horse, the bull, and the bullfighter was powerful and strange. You can see these feelings expressed in the picture.

Max Ernst's weird picture of an elephant, *Celebes*, picture **31**, makes use of an animal to express the strangeness of life. In spite of all we know through science and technology, much still remains unknown. Ernst makes us feel uncertainty and confusion, by creating a world that we almost recognize but that does not make sense.

Look at these three pictures in turn and see if you can decide which work of art from an earlier time is most like each of them.

Who are the artists?

John James Audubon (1785-1851) American

He was born in Haiti, and spent his youth in France. Audubon is known as the greatest naturalist-artist of North America. His drawings and paintings were used to illustrate books showing the animals and birds of different regions. His work can be seen in the books *Birds of North America* (original drawings in the New York Historical Society), and *The Viviparous Quadrupeds of North America* (incomplete work). Picture **29**, page 25.

Jan Brueghel (1568-1625) Flemish

Son of Pieter Brueghel I and brother of Pieter Brueghel II, both famous painters. He was a painter of still life, landscape, and flowers. He sometimes worked with Peter Paul Rubens, the famous Flemish painter. His works can be seen in the National Gallery, London, and at Oxford. Picture **10**, page 11.

Aelbert Cuyp (1620-91) Dutch

A painter of animals and landscape. He is known for the golden light that he created in his paintings. His works can be seen in the Netherlands and other collections around the world. Picture **25**, page 21.

Albrecht Dürer (1471-1528) German

A painter and printer who was the first artist to introduce Renaissance ideas about perspective and scientific observation to northern Europe. His works can be seen in major collections all over the world. Picture **23**, page 19.

Max Ernst (1891-1976) German

A painter who was an important member of the dada and surrealist art groups. He used prints from magazines and elsewhere to cut up and stick back together in new arrangements. His work appears in collections all over the world. Picture **31**, page 27.

Théodore Géricault (1791-1824) French

A "Romantic" painter of dramatic scenes, such as *Raft of the Medusa*, showing a shipwreck that actually happened. His work can be seen in major collections all over the world. Picture **27**, page 23.

Edward Hicks (1780-1849) American

He was a Quaker preacher and self-taught painter. He trained as a sign-painter. He is most famous for his many versions of *The Peaceable Kingdom* (see page 12). His work can be seen in New York and Philadelphia. Picture **11**, page 12 .

Sir Edwin Landseer (1802-73) English

A painter of sentimental pictures of animals. He was Queen Victoria's favorite painter. You can see his works in England. Picture **24**, page 20.

Franz Marc (1850-1916) German

Marc painted animals in bright colors and bold shapes. He was killed in action during World War I. There is a particularly good collection of his work in Munich in Germany. Cover picture.

Pablo Picasso (1881-1973) Spanish/French
Born in Malaga, Spain, he first visited Paris in 1900 and later lived permanently in France. He was one of the leading experimenters in art. With Georges Braque, he invented the style of art called cubism. Picasso was perhaps the greatest artist of the twentieth century and turned out a huge quantity of work. You can see his work in art collections in major galleries all over the world. Picture **30**, page 26.

Antonio Pisanello (1395-1455?) Italian
An important artist of the early Renaissance. He was very skilled at drawing, especially animals. His works can be seen in London and in Italy. Picture **12**, page 12.

Henri Rousseau (1844-1910) French
He was a self-taught painter of fantasy subjects, in a simple style. He was known as "Le Douanier," meaning "the customs officer," because that was his regular job. His works can be seen in Paris, New York, Zurich (Switzerland), London, and elsewhere. Picture **1**, page 4.

George Stubbs (1724-1806) English
A painter of portraits, animals, and landscape. He is famous for his amazing study of anatomy (the structure of bodies) and particularly for the anatomy of horses. You can see his works in major galleries and museums in Britain. Picture **26**, page 42.

Paolo Uccello (1397-1475) Italian
An early Renaissance artist, famous for his study of perspective and foreshortening. His works can be seen in Florence (Italy), Paris, and London. Picture **22**, page 19.

Sir Anthony Van Dyck (1599-1641) Flemish
He was born in Antwerp, Flanders, and as a teenager worked as chief assistant to Rubens (see Jan Brueghel). He traveled in England and Italy before settling in Flanders. His works can be seen in galleries throughout the world. Picture **24**, page 20.

Glossary

Aboriginal Relating to the native Australian people.

Acropolis The defended fort in an ancient Greek city, usually on the highest ground available.

Ancestors Family members who are no longer alive, such as great-grandparents and their parents and grandparents.

Booty Stolen goods and valuables.

Bronze A type of metal, made from copper and tin and used for making tools and sculpture.

Christian Someone who practices Christianity, the religion based on the teachings of Jesus Christ.

Creation In the Bible, God's act of bringing the Universe into being.

Crucifix A cross, or image of a cross, with an image of Jesus Christ upon it.

Cultures The ideas, beliefs, and traditions of different social groups.

Dada A movement in art that was a response to the horrors of World War I (1914-18). The aim of dada was to shock and outrage people.

Domestic Having to do with the home or ordinary life.

Figure In pictures this usually means a person or a body.

Foreground The nearest part of a scene or picture.

Foreshortening The way something seems to get smaller as it goes away from the viewer.

Genre Painting that shows people doing everyday activities.

Inuit People living in the far north of North America or northeastern Asia. Sometimes called Eskimos.

Landscape A picture of the countryside sometimes including buildings.

Media The types of paint and techniques used by artists.

Middle Ages The period of European history between the end of the Roman Empire and the Renaissance, from about A.D. 500 to 1500.

Miniature A very small painting.

Mosaic A picture or pattern made by setting small pieces (usually of stone or glass) into a floor or a wall.

Mythology A collection of myths–traditional stories usually about gods or nature. Myths are important in all cultures, giving shape to people's shared beliefs.

Oil paint A type of paint in which the color is held together with linseed or poppy seed oil. It is usually painted on wood panels, or canvas stretched on a frame. It can be used in layers with different thicknesses and textures.

Perspective The method of showing objects nearer to or farther away from the viewer. Renaissance artists developed a system for this, in which an imaginary framework is drawn first. The framework shows how objects fit together in the picture, getting smaller as they go farther away from the viewer.

Plundering Seizing and taking away peoples' belongings.

Portrait A picture of a person intended to be a record of what they look like.

Prehistoric Belonging to the time before records were kept of people and events.

Quaker A member of a Christian religious group called The Society of Friends.

Realistic Having a believable appearance.

Relief A picture that is raised, or partially three-dimensional.

Renaissance In the sixteenth century, the rediscovery in Europe of ideas from ancient Greece and Rome.

Still life A painting or drawing of objects such as flowers, fruit, books, etc.

Surrealism The surrealist movement developed from Dada (see p. 30). Surrealist art is characterized by strange images, which may include fragments of dreams and memories.

Symbol Something that represents, or stands for, something else, especially an idea.

Tapestry A decorative hanging for walls, made by weaving a picture into the material.

Totem An animal or object that a family or group of people, especially the Native Americans, adopt as their special symbol or badge. A totem pole shows off the images of a tribe's totems.

Watercolor A type of paint that is mixed with water. It is usually painted on paper, and can only be painted in thin layers, which are usually transparent.

Woodcut A print made by cutting areas of a block of wood, to form a picture. When the block is covered with ink and pressed onto paper, the cut design is printed.

Zapotec An early civilization based at Monte Alban, near Oaxaca, in present-day Mexico.

Books to read

Animals: Through the Eyes of Artists, by Wendy and Jack Richardson (Chicago: Childrens Press, 1991).

Come Look with Me: Animals in Art, by Gladys S. Blizzard (Charlottesville, Va.: Thomasson-Grant, 1992).

History of Art for Young People, by H.W. Janson and Anthony F. Janson (New York: Abrams, 4th ed., 1992).

Picture This: A First Introduction to Paintings, by Felicity Woolf (New York: Doubleday, 1989).

Understanding Modern Art, by Monica Bohm-Duchen and Janet Case (London: Usborne, 1991).

A Young Painter: The Life and Paintings of Weng Yani--China's Extraordinary Young Artist. (New York: Scholastic, 1991).

Index

Picture acknowledgments

The publishers have attempted to contact all copyright holders of the illustrations in this book, and apologize if there have been any oversights.

The photographs in this book were supplied by: Ashmolean Museum, 19(top); Bridgeman Art Library cover, 10(lower), 11, 12(top), 18, 20, 25, 26; Bruce Coleman 13(lower); ET Archive 4, 7, 8(top), 13(top), 17(top), 19(lower), 22, 27; Eye Ubiquitous/L. Fordyce 16(lower); Michael Holford 5, 6, 8(lower), 9, 14, 16(top); National Gallery 12(lower), 21, 23; Ronald Sheridan Library 10(top), 16(top), 17(lower); Tate Gallery 24; Wayland Picture Library 15. *Celebes* by Max Ernst on page 27 appears by kind permission of the copyright holders ADAGP/SPADEM, Paris and DACS, London 1992; and *The Bullfight*, Death of the Bull by Pablo Picasso, by DACS, London 1992.